God's Perspective Keys To Building Healthy Relationships and Living an Abundant Life

By Trina Bruner Jerry

No part of this publication may be reproduced, stored, or transmitted in any form or by any means, electronic, mechanical, photocopying, recording, scanning, or otherwise, except as permitted under Section 107 or 108 of the 1976 United States Copyright Act without the prior written permission of the author. Requests to the author or publisher for permission should be addressed to the following email:inspire.by.trinajerry@gmail.com

Limit of liability/disclaimer of warranty:
While the publisher and author have used their best efforts in preparing this guide, they make no representation or warranties with respect to the accuracy or completeness of the contents of this document and specifically disclaim any implied warranties of merchantability or fitness for particular purpose. No warranty may be created or extended by sales representatives, promoters, or written sales materials.
The advice and strategies contained herein may not be suitable for your situation. You should consult with a professional where appropriate.

Neither the publisher nor the author shall be liable for any loss of profit or any other commercial damages, including but not limited to special, incidental, consequential, or other damages.
Copyright© 2021

Acknowledgements

I would like to acknowledge my sister, Andrea and Keith, for supporting me in the things I aspire to do. My husband (Pitbull), my children (Tameea, Brandon, and Ryan) for putting up with me and all my flaws, my family for their support and to my co-workers that have encouraged me to follow my dreams.

Thanks To Sparkle Green-Smith for helping me to write again.

Thanks to my cover designer Bianca Brown.

Table of Contents

INTRODUCTION 1

Chapter 1- OVERVIEW OF PERSPECTIVES 4

Chapter 2 – RELATIONSHIPS AND DYSFUNCTIONAL HABITS 21

Chapter 3 - FORGIVENESS 36

Chapter 4 - MASTERING EMOTIONS 40

Chapter 5 - GETTING TO KNOW GOD 47

Chapter 6 - THE SUPERNATURAL ENCOUNTERS I HAVE HAD 55

Chapter 7 - REQUIREMENTS TO SPIRITUAL GROWTH 67

Chapter 8 - BREAKING THE PATTERN OF UNHEALTHY RELATIONSHIPS 71

Chapter 9 –THE IMPORTANCE OF THE TRUTH 86

Chapter 10 - A ROCK-SOLID MINDSET 91

Chapter 11 - BREAKING THE PATTERN OF AN UNHEALTHY MINDSET 93

Conclusion 96

References 98

INTRODUCTION

What is your definition of a healthy relationship, and what types of relationships have affected your life? My experiences have been different across the board with many bad experiences and some great ones.

There have been many people who have not experienced true love. You may have interactions with your parent(s). Your birth may have been planned or an unexpected delivery. The type of relationships you have with other people begins here with your parent(s).

Some people grow up being self-serving; never giving care to what happens to a person when they don't know how to love. Love is getting to understand and appreciate your friendships. Even God in the Bible tells us he wants friendship.

John 15:13-15

13 *Greater love hath no man than this, that a man lay down his life for his friends.*

14 *Ye are my friends if ye do whatsoever I command you.*

15 *Henceforth I call you not servants; for the servant knoweth not what his Lord doeth: but I have called you friends; for all things that I have heard of my Father I have made known unto you.*

I want this book to help people (at all times) to think about how the effect of their actions is delivered to other people. How we live our life is not just relative to us. We are prone to bring forth a selfish nature if we don't learn the act of love. Love is cultivated by learning how to properly show it. If you take the time to discern every thought that comes to mind, you will have mastered the art of love.

We help each other improve by being true to one another. I am not talking about abusing each other to try to get your point across but to actively put forth your best effort. We must put forth our best effort to be kind, unselfish, loyal to others, and honest.

Chapter 1- OVERVIEW OF PERSPECTIVES

One of my negative experiences was running out the door with intense fear. My sister and I had been told to come home at a particular time, and we were late. Our mother was furious. She pulled out the gun and pointed it at us. I ran out the door of our house. I began to hide behind cars trying to protect myself. I thought about the other time I was late, and my mother got angry and threw the knife and cut my leg. At that time, she seemed to have good aim at throwing knives. I thought about that when she pulled the gun out. I ran off in fear. I did not want to get shot in my back or leg. I had a fear of death, so I tried to find cover, hoping she was not still after me. I stayed there for some time until I was brave enough to go back home. My sister did not run; she had remained in the house.

After I returned, my sister told me I should not have run out of the house. I told her "You are crazy she likes you better than she likes me." After that incident, my mother never pulled the gun out on my sister or me again. My sister had stayed in the house and told my mother she should be ashamed of herself for doing that because she knew she was not going to shoot anyone. I, on the other hand, was not sure of that because she had thrown the knife and cut me on my leg.

I am not saying my mother was bad; she had been through a lot growing up. She was the firstborn child in her family; she was born in 1924.

She also lived when black people were picking cotton. She was not allowed to use the same bathrooms or water fountains as white people. I remember some of it myself. She was not treated well by her family. We were not even acknowledged when we visited. We were told to sit and be quiet. I cannot even remember my grandparents talking to me. My mother did not tolerate her children not following her instructions. We had many good times with our mother. She made sure we had everything we needed. Our mother wanted us to be safe. She did not want us to do things that would cause us harm. She did not want us to be treated like her family had treated her. When she had her first child, her family took over her child and would not give the child back to her.

She loved fashion and dressed very well. She was an extremely hard worker and worked in a wood plant before and after my father passed from a heart attack. She also took us to the county fair and Six Flags amusement park. She would make food and pack it for us to take to save money.

When my younger sister got married, I remember we had a marvelous time. Our mother danced so much and was extremely happy. She was a great dancer and could catch on quickly to the new dances that were out. I remember her trying to show me a dance called the scissors. I never learned how to do that dance properly. All our family had a great time, and we all danced along with our mother. And when she was eighty years plus, she was at another event and out danced everyone there. We had many great times with my mother. God blessed her with a long life. She lived to be ninety-one.

Because we were not able to have a close relationship with our grandparents, it was hard on us. We talked about it a lot. We had many ups and downs with our relationships with other people. A closer relationship with my grandparents, uncles, and aunts would have helped me have better relationship skills. There are relationship barriers that have held me back in the prior years of my life. I am working on being a better grandparent presently because of how I feel about not getting to communicate and get support from my grandparents on my mother's side of the family.

My father's mother was different; we had better communication with her, but I don't remember my grandfather. He was deceased.

My father's mother was nice to us. She lived in a small trailer home. It was not that nice of a home as I remember. It did not have an inside bathroom. When we went to her house and needed to use the restroom, there was an outhouse in the back of her home. We were afraid to go inside the wooden outhouse bathroom. We did not understand why my grandmother would not let our father buy her a better house to live in; she refused to move.

I had some great experiences with my father; we went with my father to work sometimes. He owned a cab stand business. We played checkers and dispatched calls for the cab stand. There was a blind man named Mr. Chambers that worked their dispatching calls. He would let my sister and myself receive calls some of the time. He had very keen senses because of being blind. He would know when we were around by our smell or by some other way that I am not aware of.

My father was an extremely hard worker, and he worked from morning until late at night to provide for our family. He did not properly care for his health and passed away from a heart attack. If at least one person was trained in CPR, I thought he could have possibly been saved. My sister told me they said he had a massive heart attack and that it was not possible for him to be saved.

I had a great relationship with my grandmother's sister; she was my aunt Maggie who we stayed with a lot. She was our caregiver when our father and mother worked. She was a very light-skinned woman. She looked like a white woman. I will say that she was a black woman that could pass as being white. My sister and I would be with her, and people would ask her why she had the little nigger chaps with her. Or they would ask us why we were with that white woman. My sister later told me she wondered what white woman they were referring to because she was our aunt. We were not old enough yet to understand how the color of a person's skin can affect their life. My aunt had two children; her son was dark-skinned, and her daughter was light-skinned with some color. My great aunt Beaufort never had any children. I believe she did not want to chance having a dark-skinned child. Her brother probably had a hard time growing up because of his darker skin.

The relationships that we have are significant. We must acquire excellent communication skills. My sister and I were in seclusion most of the time. We had two friends we were allowed to be around growing up.

One of our friends had many struggles in life. It was hard to watch her go through life seemingly needing attention and wanting someone to care about her. When some people go through continuous struggles, it is hard for them to live in peace, get any care to their wounds, heal the unseen injury to their heart, and endure the scars from life's abuse. People are misguided on how to apply love in everyday life toward one another. When people don't know how to love, they grow up being self-serving, never giving care to what happens to others.

Our friend had numerous encounters with some of our peers; they would want to fight with her, sometimes following her to our house wanting to fight. Another time a couple of girls tried to set up a fight after school. My sister and I told her we have time to leave and go home. We told her if she decided to stay when the fight starts, we would not help her. She refused to leave, and they did fight with her. We had said we were not getting in it and had to watch as they beat her up.

I was close to her and went to church with her. She was a member of a holiness church. I visited her church that was quite different from the church I belonged to; I remember when the church service was over, the members would greet each other with a hug. At my home church, we did not end our services that way; we would, at the most, shake the hand of the pastor as we were leaving. I would tense up every time they would try to hug me, as I was not accustomed to that kind of affection. Later in my life, I was able to accept a hug without being uncomfortable. I will talk more about our experiences with my friend in a later chapter. A look into a person's heart will help them live a life of abundance, prosperity, and good health.

I will be using the second definition of perspective: A particular attitude toward or way of regarding something; a point of view, outlook, standpoint, position, stance, attitude, the frame of mind, way of looking or thinking, vantage, point or interpretation of something (New Oxford American Dictionary).

I want to write about some of the perspective keys of life. The first thing would be being born into this world.

What happens after that?

A child is born into the world, not knowing a lot, needing help, attention, nurturing, guidance, support, and the main thing I would say is love. These ingredients will be the foundation of attitude and personality. What is needed to produce the significance of the character of a person?

The Bible tells us in Psalm 51:5

Behold, I was shapen in iniquity, and in sin did my mother conceive me.

(After the fall of Adam and Eve, we all fell under this)

I want to write about what I think the perspective keys to life are. Psalm 51:5 says I was shapen and born in iniquity. If we observe what is needed for a baby, it will need to be taken care of. They cannot walk, talk, or do anything that will nurture them on their own.

The first foundational key would be nurturing and is experienced in a great parent-child relationship. How well people do with this action will mold the personality of the child. Lives begin to bond with emotional support or neglect. Stability of relationships will build upon healthy or negative interaction. The relationship either builds character or ruins personality.

The first key in nurturing the relationship is to provide a safe and happy environment for the child. To be taught how to function correctly in life by learning positive things. It is important to be told right from wrong. It is learned by experience and interaction with others. Learning to be positive or negative may come from life experiences and initiatives.

The Bible tells us to honor your father and mother that your days be long on the earth. And then it tells parents not to provoke their children to wrath. Most of the time, people say what the children should do without saying or doing what God has told them about not provoking their children. Everyone needs to know what is required to help children learn about how they should be treated and how other people should be treated in general.

It can, at times, be hard not to go overboard when disciplining children. The choice of becoming a parent should not be a selfish decision.

The everyday interaction between parent and child is the first foundational key.

    A. Do your absolute best to be a great parent. Teach the difference between right and wrong actions they do.

    B. Never overlook selfish actions from the child.

    C. Be truthful about everything. Never assume they know what to do. Communication is essential.

    D. Help them build great relationships.

The second key is to help develop the initiative and drive and the willingness to put forth the effort to do their best at whatever they are doing.

A. Are they willing to do the work?

B. Are they willing to put forth the effort to be proficient?

C. Are they willing to study when necessary?

D. Are they willing to care about what they are doing and how it affects others?

The third key is to get understanding: The Bible tells us with all your getting, get understanding.

A. You need to be willing to find the information, to study, listen, and retain formidable information to further help you do better

B. You need to fine-tune your communication skills to be able to function with all types of people

C. Never think you know it all. There will forever be the possibility for you to learn more or improve

D. You need to pray for the ability to understand without confusion

Chapter 2 – RELATIONSHIPS AND DYSFUNCTIONAL HABITS

We should always try to improve our relationships with others and work on our communication skills. Get to know a person and hope they want the best for you and you for them. Relationships can get complicated when dealing with emotions.

There are many things that happen to people when growing up. Some may have been neglected, abused, or not told some of the essential things about life. These things will make it complicated. Mental illness can cause much trouble also. Mental illness is something that happened to a couple of people in my family. I may write a book about mental illness at a later time. At times people carry over bad habits that happened to them.

I remember being told to come home at a certain time. When I was late my mother was truly angry. She picked up a knife and was going to throw it at me, so I ran side to side trying to keep from getting hit by the knife, needless to say, it did not work because I was cut on my right leg and learned at that time to be more attentive about being home on time. Later on, in my life, she pulled the gun on me.

As I expressed in my introduction, my mother did pull a gun on me many times. I believe that to be the final time she did this to me. My sister stood up to her and refused to run. She told her that she should be ashamed of herself, and that stopped her from pulling the gun on my sister and me. She had pulled it out on some of my brothers and sisters before, but these instances finally ceased. She was at times in her life in a protective mode. If she felt in any danger, she would defend herself. Later on in life, she even pulled the gun on my daughter for coming to her house late at night; she was talking to me about it recently.

My daughter said, *"Grandma went away when I asked her for the money; she came back with the gun and pointed at me. She told me not to ever come back to her house late at night again, I almost decided not to take the money but needed it, so I took it. However, I never went back to her house late at night again."*

My uncle was not a nice man to me and my younger sister. He was extremely mean and nasty toward us. We never understood why a person would be so unkind to anyone. He never got married or had children. I believe this was a disconnect for him, and it caused him to react like this in his relationship with us. It seemed he was angry all the time. We dreaded the trips to visit because of him.

There are many dysfunctional relationships. You may encounter a person who is angry all the time, people that have a buildup of hurt within. We have to learn how to deal with and help these people.

There are bad habits that people need to work on. Emotional pain brought on by life experiences can cause wounds, bruises the heart, and can make a person unstable emotionally.

When I was younger, my sister and I had two friends that we were close to. One was a noticeably light skin black girl with gray eyes, and she had a tough time with other females. The fact that she was the only child her parents had may have contributed to some of her interactions with others.

I don't know if it were jealousy or just people being nasty just because they could that made our peers harass her. We were taught not to pick or harass people. My mother told us that you should never pick at people or mistreat them. That was a part of the information that I believe some of the people around us did not hear from their parent or parents. There was harassment continually, and there was always someone wanting to fight her, never-ending conflict.

I am ashamed to know that some people seem to have no compassion for other people. A need for someone to care for her or to need attention carried over into her adult life. Being an only child seemed to hinder her from some of the vital communication skills. Having siblings helped us to deal with conflict, learn to share, not be selfish and self-serving, and have support from one another in a difficult situation. There were many forms of support given.

My mother gave birth to ten children, and that was in itself, probably a challenge at times. All people need to build on better relationship skills with every interaction they have. Every relationship you have is unique and should be treated uniquely.

On the other side of things, my daughter was darker-skinned and had problems with being darker. So, my friend had issues being too light-skinned and my daughter had problems being too dark.

There have been many instances that have happened in the past and in this present time. The first instance I will refer to is the killing of a young boy named Emmett Louis Till. He was murdered at 14 years of age because of racial discrimination against him. He was accused of offending a white woman by whistling at her. He was treated like he was not a human being.

Emmett was visiting family members down south in Money, Mississippi, in 1955. Emmett was from Chicago, Illinois. He was lynched while visiting for summer vacation.

Emmett's accuser told her husband of the whistling incident and he and his half-brother went looking for the boy three days later. They had said they were going to teach him a lesson. Emmett was later found murdered.

Later in her life, his accuser said that she did not tell the full truth about what Emmett had done. She had added to what truly happened.

You can look up information about his life on the internet. And there is information about his mother also on YouTube. His mother's name is, Mamie Carthan Till Mobley.

Mamie Till Mobley (Mamie Till Speaks of Forgiveness) on YouTube.

There should be no one that exists that should not know what happened to this young man.

And in this current time of last year, 2020, we have had too many instances of the same nature where black people have lost their life unexpectedly because of their race.

It has been stated that police have killed 164 black people in the first eight months of 2020; because of this happening, the reason for these actions occurring over and over again should be looked into.

These are a few people who were killed for various reasons. Rayshard Brooks 27, Daniel Prude 41, George Floyd 46, Breonna Taylor 26, Atatiana Jefferson 28, Aura Rosser 40, Stephon Clark 22, Botham Jean 26, Philando Castille 32, Alton Sterling 37, Michelle

Casseavx 50, Freddie Gray 25, Janisha Fonville 20, Eric Garner 43, Akai Gurley 28, Gubriella Nevurez 22, Michael Brown 18, Tanisha Anderson 37, and Tamir Rice 12 years old. Tamir was shot while holding a toy gun.

If these instances are not enough to let all people know that race relation needs to be looked into, I don't know what is wrong with the consciousness of the people in this world. There is much work that needs to occur about racial problems and hate in this country and around the world.

In the Jim crow era, there was a song. The words to it stated: *If you're white, it's alright if you're brown stick around, but if you're black, oh brother, get back, get back, get back.*

It is the -Big Bill Broonzy: Black, Brown, and White(HaloedG) YouTube

(BibleGateway.com) Genesis 2:18 KJV-*And the Lord God said it is not good that man be alone. I will make him an help meet for him.* So, in general, it is not suitable for any of us to be alone. People need to communicate with others because isolation is not a good thing.

1. <u>Codependent</u>

There can be a codependent relationship where the person relies solely on the other person to function. If they do not receive directions from that person, they cannot move forward. People must learn to be independent in most of the decisions they make by learning to make positive choices and being able to determine on their own what would be the right thing to do without being influenced by anyone else.

An example would be if you find yourself in a situation where you might get in a lot of trouble or would go to jail because of something your friend wants you to do, and you decide on your own to tell him, or her that you cannot do what they are asking you to do and you walk away. You have made a proper decision. Learn to be independent, not a follower.

2. <u>Bullying or Abusive Relationships</u>

There can be bullying in some relationships. Bullying usually starts with school-age children. A person attacks a person because they do not like them for some reason or are doing it because of peer pressure, showing out, or just because they have not been taught better. A husband or wife can bully their partner; there is often no respect toward one another. There can be abuse in marriages. It can come from both sexes.

3. <u>Parental Mirroring</u>

There can also be parental mirroring. When a person behaves as their parent did, they follow in the footsteps of the parent without meaning to. I find myself at times getting angry and cursing even though I hated it when my mother uttered profanity a lot, especially when she was mad about something. I learned to block her out.

When she would curse most of the day, I would not hear her. I have heard it many times when a person makes a promise that they will not act like their parents did but then fail utterly.

Keys to dealing with dysfunctional relationships

    A. Learn to be kind and show love.

    B. Care about other people's feelings and work on bad habits by owning up to the things you know are wrong to do.

    C. Treat others as you would like to be treated by fine-tuning your communication skills.

    D. Deal with conflict positively.

Biblegateway.com 7:12 KJV

Matthews 7:12

12 Therefore all things whatsoever ye would that men should do to you, do ye even so to them: for this is the law of the prophets.

Chapter 3 - FORGIVENESS

To forgive is an act of kindness that will help you and the other person move toward healing. To let go of resentment from being hurt, slighted, offended, abused, or angered.

Forgiveness is something we all must master because of being a requirement from God according to the Bible. (BibleGateway.com) Matthew 6:14-15 tell us about forgiving others so our Heavenly Father will also forgive us. It tells us if we do not forgive others we will not be forgiven.

Forgiving is so important to us because unforgiveness can cause us much trouble. It can affect our emotions and our health. (Proverbs 14:30) tells us that envy is rottenness to the bones. So, envy causes infection to our heart health. Envy means that you are jealous or desire what someone else has because you don't have it. People need to master how they react to others and the things they have. The Bible tells us that out of the heart flows the issues of life, so it is essential what we accept in our hearts as far as love or hate. We should try our absolute best to have positive thoughts rather than negative ones.

We should guard our hearts with all diligence, just as we are to take every thought captive.

When we are concerned about our thoughts, we put our communication skills into action. When we control holding on to grudges and resentment about the things that have hurt us, we can easily forgive when we refer back to the Bible. The Bible tells us to be angry and sin not. The Bible also instructs us that we should not let the sun go down if you have not dealt with whatever the problem you have had.

People can have built-up hurt by some of the things that have happened to them growing up. One could be the passing of a family member or a friend; they feel sorrow about their loss.

There can be a different action if a person is deceased because of the negative effect of another person, such as an accident where a drunk driver has caused a death, or a person has lost their life to stabbing or gunshot incident. I have heard people say I can never forgive that person for the death. It could even be caused by being mistreated by family, friends, or even strangers.

The forgiveness level of people varies because some people may forgive easier than another person.

(BibleGateway.com Ephesians 4:26)

Be ye angry, and sin not: let not the sun go down upon your wrath.

Chapter 4 - MASTERING EMOTIONS

When a child is born, they have an emotional attachment to their mother. They know that is their parent. They acquire bonding with their mother. The friendship begins at that time. Emotions are feelings; they can be happy, unhappy, angry, or excited every time they come in contact with their mother. They also bond with their father if he is there from the beginning. If he is not, they will bond later by learning to trust their father.

Depending on how you raise them, they could become spoiled if you do not let them interact with other people. They will cry when another person picks them up, having separation anxiety.

My daughter would cry when I was coming to pick her up at the daycare. When she heard my footsteps, she knew I was coming and would cry until I got to her.

As we teach our children to deal with everyday life, we should be concerned about how they react to people. Our children learn by interacting with others. They have to learn how to communicate with their parents, siblings, friends, and others they may have a great experience or a conflict with. Children sometimes will show selfish tendencies. They will not want to share toys or things they consider theirs. A parent should let them know that this is not how they should react to these situations. With my children and grandchildren, I would call it my syndrome, acting as if everything belongs to them. I would have to tell them that it was not so and tell them about sharing, caring, and understanding how to treat others and not to covet things. Coveting something is wanting what someone else has that does not belong to you. A person would need to be told not to act that way. If they want something, they need to work toward getting the same thing.

Mastering emotions is learning to properly deal with the situation before you. If you have a desire or want something or if you come up against some conflict, you will need to be able to make reasonable decisions at all times. There are many emotions that a person can have that can be positive or negative.

Positive emotions, joy, peace, and happiness come about when you feel good about yourself. Hopefully, you have had great experiences with other people when you learn to deal with everyday positive situations.

The keys to mastering coping skills:

A. You would need to know that things may not go how you want them to go, so you would need to learn acceptance without being resentful.

B. You would need to properly deal with conflicts, loss, hurt, and anger that can arise if a thing does not go your way.

C. Good character is cultivated by making wise decisions; how you deal with everyday situations is important.

D. You have to master love. If you are devoted to something or someone you care about it or the person's feelings, you would not want to do anything that would hurt or cause harm. Trust needs to be established.

Positive emotions, I believe, are beneficial to good health. Negative emotions bring to people a load of troubles they do not need to carry. When they can release negative emotions, then good things will be replaced by letting good produce.

(BibleGateway.com) *Galatians 5:22-23(KJV)*

22 But the fruit of the Spirit is love, joy, peace, long-suffering, gentleness, goodness, faith,

23 Meekness, temperance: against such is no law.

Discernment is a gift; it is a knowledge and determination of what is the best action to make in the decision-making process in making reasonable decisions.

Ignoring negative feelings is not a good thing. Anger, resentment, jealousy, depression, and fear are emotions that need to be dealt with. We have been told to take every thought captive that comes against good.

(BibleGateway.com 2 Corinthians 10:5(KJV)

5 Casting down imaginations, and every high thing that exalteth itself against the knowledge of God and bringing into captivity every thought to the obedience of Christ.

The negative emotions pollute the heart. We have been told that out of our hearts flow the issues of life.

Chapter 5 - GETTING TO KNOW GOD

The Bible tells us that God is a spirit, and those that worship Him must worship in spirit and truth. God is someone that we have been told no one has seen. If you read about Moses, it tells us in the Bible that he only saw the backside of God. The Bible tells us about The Father (God), Son (Jesus), and The Holy Spirit. We all need to read the Bible and ask for an understanding of this.

How do we communicate with God? One way is to pray. You can write to God, talk to Him, and ask Him questions and listen for answers. God communicates with us in many ways. You may have a dream, some people have a vision, (open vision), and someone may get insight to come tell you something, or to give you something. You might have a special feeling or know when you should do or not do something. Ask God for insight and understanding. And give thanks in all things.

Bible Gateway Matthew 6:33

33 But seek ye first the kingdom of God and his righteousness, and all these things will be added unto you.

John 15:7 King James Version (KJV)

7 If ye abide in me and my words abide in you, you can ask what you will, and it will be done unto you.

The Bible tells us to study to show ourselves approved and to let the word of God be written on the tables of our hearts. We should read the Bible and ask for an understanding of it. The Bible is here for inspiration for us as God's people and will help us to have spiritual growth. Many people reject any concept that there could be any force beyond what we can see.

John 3:16 said: *God so loved the world that He gave His only begotten son that whosoever believes in Him shall not perish but have everlasting life.* God sent Jesus in the world to live the human experience.

There are names that many refer to God such as:

ELOHIM: My Creator

JEHOVAH: My Lord God

EL SHADDAI: My Supplier

ADONAI: My Master

JEHOVAH JIREH: My Provider

JEHOVAH ROPHE: My Healer

JEHOVAH NISSI: My Banner

JEHOVAH MAKADESH: My Sanctifier

JEHOVAH TSIDKENU: My Righteousness

JEHOVAH SHALOM: My Peace

JEHOVAH ROHI: My Shepherd

JEHOVAH SHAMMAH: My Abiding Presence

YESHUA (Hebrew) name for JESUS

JESUS My Lord

The keys to getting to know God is to:

    A. Ask Him to help you have an understanding

B. Read the Bible. It is said to be spirit and truth

C. Love God with all your heart

D. Treat other people as if you are doing it for God

At the last supper, God said He had a greater commandment for us to do. And it was to show love in everything we do.

I say mastering love is the very essence of God

John 3:16 said: God so loved the world that He gave His only begotten son that whosoever believes in him shall not perish but have everlasting life. God sent Jesus in the world to live the human experience. I believe He was trying to find out what made man struggle so much with making the right decisions. It was relevant and necessary to be able to forgive us for sin. If you begin to read, you may understand what I am talking about.

God has promised to be here for us to never withhold any good thing from us. It would benefit us all to be aware of the things he has promised to us. The gift of the Holy Spirit is one promise we should seek. We can have a relationship with the Holy Spirit and learn to listen and hear Him. The Holy Spirit was sent so that everyone would always have access to Him. It is up to every believer to accept the gift of The Holy Spirit because it is available to us all for the taking. We can reject the instructions given by Him in our everyday choices.

There are so many promises that I cannot name them all.

The stubborn nature of man keeps some of us from moving forward in life. By reading the Bible, we can get a better understanding of the personality of God by gaining an understanding of the things Jesus did. It is the essence of the changes made when God sent His son.

(BibleGateway.com) John 3:16

16 For God so loved the world, that he gave his only begotten Son, that whosoever believeth in him should not perish, but have everlasting life.

God wants to have a close relationship with us and wants us to communicate with Him regularly, through prayer, trust, believing, and faith.

Life's Lessons in Poems (Trina Lavette Bruner) 2002 page 29

God speaks to me:

God speaks to me each and every day,

He speaks to me in many different ways,

When I start to do something wrong,

He lets my conscience have its way.

He speaks to me through people,

Inspiring in them just what to say.

And if I listen carefully, I'll do it the right way.

I know that God speaks to me

And that you might disagree.

But I say God speaks to me, even when I'm asleep.

Over the high and mighty mountains

I know he speaks

Across the sea on soaring waves

I know he speaks

When I see the lightening in the sky

I know he speaks

When I hear the thunder roar,

I know he speaks

I speak to him.

He speaks to me.

Chapter 6 - THE SUPERNATURAL ENCOUNTERS I HAVE HAD

The first time I had a supernatural encounter, I was a young child. My father was still alive at that time and in my life. I was not paying attention and walked out into the road. When I did the car hit me, I flew up into the air then hit the ground. I did not have even a scar on me from the incident. I believe angels or God protected me. My father came and was frantic that I was hit by the car but was happy I was not injured.

The second time was after my father died. I was sitting in a chair in the living room of the house we grew up in. As I was sitting there that night, I saw my father over the fireplace. I also saw Jesus. It was not a full body of them. As I sat there, I did not say anything. I was not afraid of seeing them; I just looked at them. I thought to myself that they were watching over me. I did not tell anyone what had happened to me because of how unbelievable it might sound. I felt comfortable knowing that I was being watched over.

The third encounter occurred when I was a member of a Holiness Church. I saw a vision of a church. As I looked at the church, I saw it fall to the ground. Then I wondered what it meant. While I was thinking of the vision, something inside me told me that the Church I belonged to would have a falling away, meaning that people would leave the church because of many different reasons. This did happen more than once.

The fourth encounter I had was in the holiness church I had joined. Earlier in my life, I got pregnant before I had my last child. I came to find myself pregnant again and was having a hard time thinking I could raise another child. I talked to the father of the child, and we decided that it would be best to abort the child. The father of the child gave me the money, and I had a friend of mine go with me to the abortion clinic. I had an abortion and went on with my life. I reunited with my last child's father, and our son was conceived and born shortly after. Later I got pregnant again; it may seem like a strange thing, but I knew that I would be pregnant at the very moment that it happened. I felt the conception when it happened. I got a test, and it was positive. I, again in my mind, was thinking I cannot take care of any more children and decided to have another abortion. I had it and began to believe that God would never forgive me for having two abortions. I would not forgive myself for it and was struggling with what I had done. I could not move forward spiritually but continued to go to church. One Sunday, I had an experience at the church. I was under the power of the anointing, and I heard the voice of God. It sounded like He was talking through many waters. I heard God tell me that the children were with Him. It let me know that the children I had were children at conception. I think God let me know this so I could move on with my life and let go of the fear that I could never be forgiven for what I had done. After that experience, my pastor told me that she felt the anointing as it was happening to me. The power of God is real, and the supernatural is also. I am sure of this because of the experiences I have had. I believe that God loves us all and wants us to make better decisions in our life. He is a forgiving God.

To you mothers out there that have had an abortion or abortions, I would like for you to know that the children are in heaven, and they are with God.

The fifth encounter I had was at church. My friend's mother had a praise dance, and I admired the dance. I prayed that God would let me have the same kind of dance. Later on, my prayer was answered. I did get to dance as she had danced. One Sunday, as I was dancing, I almost fell. I guess if I had fallen, I would have been severely injured, so I had a supernatural experience. Instead of falling, something kept me from hitting the floor or any other object, and I was lifted without touching the floor and moved to the other side of the room, landing on my feet. As I landed, I thought about Angels keeping me in all my ways, lest I dash my foot against a stone (Psalm91).

The sixth encounter was when I went to a church out of town. When I was there, I went up for prayer. While up there, I fell under the power of the Holy Spirit. When I came up under control yielding to the Holy Spirit, I heard the Spirit saying He loved a young lady. As this was happening, I was saying to myself that I hoped the Lord loved me too. After that, the church members started treating me differently. They acted like they did not understand why I would be the one used in that way. It seems so hard for people to accept a move of the power of God.

The seventh encounter I had was at another church. I saw an open vision of a friend. She was in a purple dress in the vision, and I heard a voice say she would have double for her trouble. (Isaiah 61:7 tells us about the people of God getting double for their trouble.) I went and told her what I saw and asked her if she understood what it meant. She said she did understand.

I have, at times, heard a voice tell me things. One day I was on my job and listened to a voice tell me to stop stonewalling. I had never heard the word before, so I asked a friend if she knew what it meant.

She laughed and told me to look up the word. I did and got a general idea of what the meaning was. That incident let me know that we do not only hear good things all of the time, but we can listen for instructions if we are not doing what is necessary to move forward in the path of our destiny. I don't know for sure the exact plans God has for me, but I am seeking answers.

I have always wanted a close relationship with God. When we were young children, we would walk to church. We would go to Sunday School first and stay for the regular Sunday service. At Sunday School, we would read the Bible and discuss how we should apply these actions to our everyday life. I always wanted to have a close relationship with God and understand the Bible.

We would listen to the preacher, and always at the end of the service, they would ask if anyone would like to give their life to the Lord. They would sing a song while calling us to worship and be born again. The song would say come to Jesus, come to Jesus, come to Jesus just now, come to Jesus come to Jesus just now.

It was a song that would draw people to the front of the church to say that they wanted to serve the Lord. They would sometimes sing a different tune. It would say, Jesus is tenderly waiting and calling, calling for you and for me, Jesus is tenderly waiting and calling, calling for sinners to come home. Come home, come home......calling for sinners to come home. The songs would draw people to go and ask to be forgiven. I would go up many times by hearing the songs. I always wondered if I was truly saved. So, I would go up many times.

I want to have a close relationship with God and have a great understanding of the Word of God. Even with all the spiritual encounters I have had, I am not sure I understand fully what I need to know to have a spiritual relationship. But one thing I know for sure is that I believe.

I had another encounter with the supernatural while at a church. I was under the power of the Holy Spirit, and I heard Him say there would be a shaking of the vine. I did not want to be out of order in the church service, so I told a member of the church to let the pastor know what God had told me. She told the pastor what I said, but they did not let the word go forth.

I started to praise the Lord again, and the power of the Holy Spirit was going to move again, but the pastor told the person that was to make the announcements to do so. Then while I was under the power of the Holy

Spirit, I was led to sit down. When I went to sit down, the church member said," you were under the power of the Holy Spirit, you should have let the word go forth." As the member said that to me, I told her I was led to sit down. Then I heard the Holy Spirit say He was a gentleman, and He did not have to talk over anyone. She seemed amazed that I said that.

After that, a young man on the other side of the church got up and put his hand out to help a person step down from the pulpit. I say that the Holy Spirit let that happen, so she would have a confirmation that it was Him. Then I heard the Holy Spirit say that they missed it.

Many people do not believe in demons, but I have had two experiences seeing a person get delivered from a demon. The first one was a woman that had a demon, and the evil spirit started to curse and refused to leave her at first. It took some time, and then the devil left her body. After that happened, her complexion looked around three shades lighter than before her deliverance.

They took pictures of her before and after that happened and then showed all of us that were there. The picture before her deliverance had two lines of light on her head, and the one after her deliverance had a circle of light. The second instance was a female also, and it took some time for her deliverance, and the woman was freed from the demon. I have not been where I have seen any more instances of a person having been possessed with a demon.

Chapter 7 - REQUIREMENTS TO SPIRITUAL GROWTH

It is important to get an understanding of your purpose; why you are here and what you can do to be a help to the world.

Self-respect, self-discipline, self-improvement may be needed to help us move forward in the things that will make our lives better.

Watching what comes from us may help us move forward. Discernment is a spiritual tool that we need to acquire.

Discernment

Noun

1. **The ability to judge well:** an astonishing lack of discernment.

2. **(in Christian contexts) perception in the absence of judgement with a view to obtaining spiritual direction and understanding** without providing for a time of healing and discernment, there will be no hope of living through this present moment without a shattering of our everyday life.

We acquire spiritual growth by applying the principles of the Bible to our everyday living. We need to read and learn what the Bible tells us to fulfill what we have been told. Examples are to be angry and sin not; do not let the sun go down if you are mad without dealing with the problem; be kind to everyone, especially to those of the household of faith, and do unto others as you would have them do unto you.

There are many other things that each person can work on such as not to have hate in our hearts toward people of a different ethnic group. Praying in the spirit can help with our spiritual growth and allowing God to renew our minds and transform our hearts.

Fear is something we need to deal with because we have not been given the spirit of fear. We can be fearful of many things, but in general, we should not be in a state of anxiety or panic. Negative emotions are in opposition to spiritual health. It brings forth spiritual decay.

A seed of love needs to be deposited in the heart of every person that has been granted the breath of life. As we move toward being the best we can be and understanding who God created us to be, we can seek to learn the character of our God.

Chapter 8 - BREAKING THE PATTERN OF UNHEALTHY RELATIONSHIPS

A predator is said to be a person or group that ruthlessly exploits influences. It is not an easy way to determine if a person is going to pursue a person in a negative way. Trust needs to be an essential factor in building relationships with other people.

When I was a young child my sister and I would always walk to church. Our parents did not go with us to church. We went to Sunday School to learn about the Bible. Our experience was a great one with a preacher named Reverend Irvis. He was a very great preacher, as I remember.

After he died, we got another preacher. He was a younger man. One day he asked me to come into his office to talk to me. When I got in there, he talked to me for a couple of minutes. After that, he came over and grabbed me. He tried to sexually assault me. I pulled away from him and ran out the side door of his office.

I ran all the way home. I never told my mother because I was afraid, she would go and shoot him. I thought she might go to jail, and we would not have a parent to live with anymore because my father had died already. I can't remember if I told my younger sister that he tried to assault me because she might tell my mother. I went back to church and made sure I was never alone with him again. He was later moved to another church.

Then we had another pastor sent to the church. He was an older preacher. One day he told me to tell my mother that we were going to a town called Love Valley to find some slave gravesites to do a project. I told her and she let me go with him.

We rode up to Love Valley but could not find the place where the slave gravesites were. We saw two white men in front of a store. He stopped and asked them where the gravesite was. They told him and we found the site.

After getting there I was leaning down and going to write down some of the names off the tombstones. As I was writing he grabbed me and tried to assault me. I jumped up and shook my finger in his face and told him. "*You take your hands off me right now and take me home.*" He took his hands off me and took me home.

I feel lucky that we had encountered the two white men and that I had told my mother that I was going with him. I feel things could have been terrible for me because he was bigger and stronger than I was and could have done whatever he wanted to do to me.

After this incident, I decided not to be so trusting of older men, and I made sure I was never alone with a preacher at a young age anymore. I am not saying I think all preachers are like these two men. However, I did not want to chance this happening again.

I feel if my parents had not told us it is wrong for a man or boy to touch or fondle you, I would have thought it was ok for the preachers to touch me. If you are not told about the possibility of coming in contact with a predator, you, as a child, will think you can trust all adults, family members, and friends. There is a broad group of possible relationships we may acquire, so there is a need to determine if you are going to have a healthy relationship with the person.

There have also been incidents where family members tried to do the same thing. I say it is important not to assume that siblings know better if they are not told differently. It is so important that parents do not assume that children automatically know right from wrong. Parents need to talk with their children and ask them questions about many subjects.

I know of instances about the abuse that happened to family members. It sometimes does not matter if it is a male or female. There was abuse from cousins from both sexes. I have heard about fathers that have assaulted their daughter or daughters, a brother, cousin, friend, uncle, and the list could have more people. Teachers have also assaulted people. Gender does not matter.

Later on in my life, I was at a public swimming pool. An older boy came over and was interested in me. He started to feel on me; in the beginning, it felt ok. I was curious about what he was doing. Then he began to try and penetrate me; it was painful. He was assaulting me in the pool. He finally let me go.

The next experience I had was when talking to a man. I had talked to him many times at the YMCA. At this time in my life, I am a grown-up now. One day he was telling me where he lived. He told me he did not want anything from me but wanted me to see his apartment.

He told me where it was, so I went to the apartment. When I got there and walked into the apartment, he grabbed me and tried to feel on me. I realized then that I had made a mistake going there. I wiggled away from him and tried to get out the door of the apartment.

He kept grabbing at me; I almost fell over the balcony because his apartment was upstairs. I did not fall over it and was able to run down the stairs. After this incident, I had learned that you have to be careful about what you listen to when dealing with people. You have to determine what their motives are when asking you to do certain things. I have had too many close calls when dealing with some of the opposite sex.

There have been many people that have been abducted, raped, held captive, and killed by making the wrong choice when encountered by some predators. You cannot tell by the look, personality, or attitude of a person, you have to be careful at all times.

When I was almost a teenager myself, and some other females were in the company of some males, they were trying to entice us with money to see body parts. I can say we fell for that. There were things going on that our parent/parents did not know about.

After I graduated, I had one of my teachers who tried to get me to have sex with him. When I would not, he got mad and tried to manipulate me by saying mean things to me. I refused to let that happen and just flat out said no.

There was a man old enough to be my father. He lived in the apartment complex I lived in. He lived a couple of houses down from me. One day he stopped me on the road. When I stopped to talk to him, he asked me to have sex with him. I was shocked and angered by him asking me that. I told him. *"You should be ashamed of yourself.*

You are old enough to be my father. I am not going to say anything to your wife, but if you ever ask me that again I will go down to your house and tell her." He never approached me like that again.

There were predators all around us. We had a man try to get us to get in his car. He would ride around and try to get us to go with him. We ran down the long driveway to tell the grown-ups about this incident.

There are countless stories about predators, and it is both male and female. Some began this type of action in their youth. Sometimes there are signs that a person may have some problems, and then there are times when you may not recognize anything because of a person concealing their actions well.

There have been many serial killers, women and men that have harmed others; some have caused harm to entire families. I could go on and on about stories I have heard, news reports, and TV shows about different people causing harm to others; some say they do not know why they do what that they do.

There are no clear explanations of why some people do these types of things. The perspective key to spotting a predator could be numerous.

    A. Caution should be used at all times when dealing with people. Use your instincts to determine if you feel anything seems wrong. Watch for signs of strange behavior and attitude.

B. You cannot always know what a person went through in their life. Some of these actions may come about by the life experiences a person had. So, be careful about building healthy relationships with everyone you come in contact with. Use your instinct to evaluate every situation. Do not look over the signs of negative behavior. If you have a terrible feeling about something, do not ignore that feeling.

C. Listen carefully when information is given about being safe in different circumstances. Children being warned about stranger danger, they should listen to what they are being told and act accordingly.

D. It is not as easy as it would seem to read a person's intentions, so ere on the side of being cautious when dealing with people. If this were an easy subject, then there would not be so many assaults, murders, child abductions, hate crimes, and many new things that can happen.

We had an encounter with a stalker. He started with phone calls, harassing us. I would answer the phone and curse him out. Later he used fear to threaten my family to get control over someone close to me. He said he would kill us and blow up our house. It was another frightening moment for me, the mental torture was a lot for me. I was wanting to move or escape from it. It was a trying time in my life.

I was not the one that he was trying to control but was still feeling the effect of what he was doing. I finally moved, and he came to my house. He had told the person that he had stalked that they needed to convince us they wanted to be with him. When I saw him, I could not believe my eyes. I thought it had to be wrong that they wanted to be with him.

My mother had come over to meet him. After that, the person that he had made the person break up with came over. When he saw him, he fell to the floor and said, *"you left me for this!"* He was flamboyant, so the man pulls out a gun. We all scattered and knocked over the furniture in my apartment. I had children at this time. They were not home at the time.

After he did that, I called the police. They came to my house. I told them he had pulled out a gun in my house. Because he was a white man, they refused to check for the gun. They would not even make him leave my home. He stayed there and would not leave. Everyone else that was in my house including my mother left and went home. I was not leaving my house with him there, so I stayed. I locked myself in my bedroom.

 In the morning I got up, took a shower, and got dressed for church. He made a comment about how nice I looked. I told him I was going to church and gave him my key to the house. I told him to please lock my door, put the key over the top of the door, and be gone when I return. He did as I had asked and was gone when I came back from church.

He harassed the person for some time after that. We finally got rid of him by having female police talk to him and threaten to put him in jail if he did not stop harassing the person. I have had many bad things happen to me, so have some of my other family members. It has been a long journey over the years.

It took some years to get rid of the stalker. I don't remember the exact time, but it seemed like an eternity.

Chapter 9 – THE IMPORTANCE OF THE TRUTH

Oxford dictionary:

truth

noun

the quality or state of being right.

"he had to accept the truth of her accusation."

The truth is fundamental in everyday life. We are encouraged by God to tell the truth.

The Bible tells us the things that God hates.

Bible Gateway: Proverbs 6:16-19 (KJV)

16 These six things doth the Lord hate: yea, seven are an abomination unto him:

17 A proud look, a lying tongue, and hands that shed innocent blood,

18 A heart that deviseth wicked imaginations, feet that be swift in the running to mischief,

19 A false witness that speaketh lies, and he that Soweth discord among the brethren.

The Bible tells us that Jesus said: *"And ye shall know the truth, and the truth shall make you free."*

It is important that we learn about the things of truth.

The things of truth will help us to live a great life. Lies and secrets can cause harm and cause havoc in a person's life.

In my book of poems, I wrote a poem titled: *Secrets and lies*

(Life's Lessons in Poems) Trina Lavette Bruner:

Secrets and Lies

Secrets and lies

Lies that are spreading like riding the tides

Spreading out, so far and so wide

Traveling fast as they can go

Lies that should have never been told

Lie at your side

Lie at your side

Your conscience should have kept you from telling those lies

Those lies can be harmful

And ruin others' lives

Messing up lives

Messing up lives

Many lives ruined by those secrets and lies

The truth of the matter is that I will do almost anything to support my children and be a support to them. We should all stand up for our own. **It has been a struggle getting what family needs to move forward with a support system.**

My daughter has had to deal with not being able to pay all of her bills and having to choose between food or shelter. Somehow this is the reality of many people in this day and time.

Integrity is essential in letting the truth be recognized and understood. It seems that not standing for what is the right thing to do is not so important these days. There are lies and confusion in our government system. Many people not receiving justice when horrible things have happened. We have had a young man get killed for just walking in a neighborhood, and another one was shot for playing music too loud in his automobile. The truth should be factual and correct. Anything else moves from fact to untrue, which runs into a lie. Truth and trust should run side by side. Dealing with trust, it needs to be established in all relationships.

We all need to guard our life with all diligence for out of our hearts flow the issues of life. The things we do to others, and the way we treat other people come directly from what is inside of us. Our upbringing and how we were taught to deal with people we come in contact with will surface by how we respond to our peers. Our heart needs to have love flowing continually. The world will be a better place when we treat each person we come in contact with love.

The first key: Be kind

The second key: Tell the truth, be honest

The third key: Treat every person with respect

The fourth key: Show love when there are controversies that need to be solved. Be kind as you can be.

The fifth key: Respect each person's rights to exist, so do no harm to other people.

Chapter 10 - A ROCK-SOLID MINDSET

When my sister and I were young girls, we went to the cab stand; my father had a taxicab business. There was another taxicab business right down the street. One of the drivers would call my sister **Little Rock**, and he called me **Big Rock**. They were kind to us even though the business was the same. They never had any conflict with the taxi companies.

In 2002 I wrote a poem about my sister:

Like a rock, you stood firm went through life without complaining

Hoping that one day you would find complete happiness

You stood strong against life's seasons

Like winter cold you felt life's pain.

With summer's warmth your life was sustained.

Against spring's winds breeze, you stood still and was thankful that you are still here to see falls beauty.

You tried to refrain from anything that would cause you pain,

But you stood firm when those pains were thrown your way

Because a rock can fair those seasons and still there remain

My sister and I have had many things happen to us in our life. We have had ups and downs but keep striving for what is best for our families.

The keys to a rock-solid mindset:

The first one is to be willing to understand. We need to obtain knowledge in many things and about many different circumstances.

The second one is to be willing to agree to disagree.

We all may have different opinions on many subjects.

The third one is to have healthy thought patterns.

Make sure you have control over negative thoughts.

The fourth one is to treat every person like you want to be treated.

Chapter 11 - BREAKING THE PATTERN OF AN UNHEALTHY MINDSET

How we break the pattern of an unhealthy mindset is to have self-control. We all need to have a positive thought process. Making wise decisions in the things we do for our family, workplace, school, church, or other engagements. Our thought process is vital while living in this world. We need to work on bad habits that we have created by learned behaviors that cause us trouble in our relationships.

The lack of control, when angry, can cause much pain for us when we have no control over our emotional state. It can cause harm to others as well as to yourself in mind, body, and soul. Some habits only affect us;

then, some affect many people. There are habits that we acquire in our family line that are learned patterns, sometimes called generational curses, following the same practices from one person in a family bloodline to the next generation. Abuse can be a real problem in relationships in many forms. Verbal and physical are two.

There can also be people who have a controlling type of attitude. They want to have full control over another person controlling where a person can go, who they can be around, how long they can be out, what they wear, and who they can talk to.

At one time in my life, I knew of a person whose husband would lock her and her children in a room. They had access to a bathroom. I never understood why she would let him treat her that way. Later in her life, she got tired of that happening and left the relationship.

There are also ethnic groups that learn to hate entire groups of people, whether they are African American, Caucasian, Asian, Hispanic, or other ethnic groups. They follow what they had learned from their family. The final key is to realize that we are the human race, and every person has the right to life and to have a chance to show great potential on this earth.

Conclusion

It is up to us all to govern our actions; it is a part of mastering self-control. God is omnipotent, meaning his existence is stable, he will forever exist, and he is all-knowing. God is my solid foundation, and I need to do everything I can to understand my purpose and why I am here on earth. I desire to have and retain information that will help me to have spiritual growth. God is a spirit, and those that worship him must worship him in spirit and truth.

Living a positive life is no easy journey to take; there are many different directions I can go and important decisions to make. It is up to me to be wise in how I live my life. If I start by mastering self-control, I will be traveling on the right road.

Master yourself and move forward in confidence that you can make the correct decisions in everyday life. Discern every thought, every action. Then make wise decisions. You may stumble as you travel but learn to make proper choices in life.

Take a journey forward to build great relationships with whomever you come in contact with. We are in charge of what happens to us when we come to an age where we can make wise decisions on our own, master it, and make smart choices. Pre-judge every situation. Ask yourself questions. If I do it this way, how will it affect me? If this happens, what negative things can cause me problems down the road?

References
Bible gateway.com John 15:13-25

New Oxford American Dictionary online: perspective

BibleGateway.com: Psalm 51:5

YouTube- Big Bill Broonzy: Black, Brown, and White

BibleGateway.com: Genesis 2:18 (KJV)

BibleGateway.com: 7:12 (KJV)

BibleGateway.com: Proverbs 14:30

BibleGateway.com: Ephesians 4:26

BibleGateway.com: Galatians 5:22-23(KJV)

BibleGateway.com: 2 Corinthians 10:5(KJV)

BibleGateway.com: Matthew 6:33(KJV)

BibleGateway.com: John 15:7(KJV)

BibleGateway.com: John 3:16

Names of God

(Life's Lessons in Poems) Trina Lavette Bruner 2002 pg. 29

Angels keeping me in all my ways

Oxford Dictionary online: Discernment

Be angry and sin not

Be kind to everyone

Do unto others as you would have them do unto you

Not given the spirit of fear

Oxford Dictionary online: Truth definition

BibleGateway.com: Proverbs 6:16-19(KJV)

(Life's Lessons in Poems) Secrets and Lies: Trina Lavette Bruner 2002 page

Mamie Till Mobley (Mamie Till Speaks of Forgiveness) on YouTube.

Poem: My Sister the Rock, Trina Bruner Jerry. Newspaper article 2002 Statesville Record and Landmark

Reflections/Thoughts